UNFOLDED CLOTHES

Why Do Women Have Unfolded Clothes?

Doris La'Shelle

UNFOLDED CLOTHES

Copyright © 2022 Doris La'Shelle

All rights reserved.

ISBN: 979-8-9857485-1-2

UNFOLDED CLOTHES

DEDICATION

To all the women who have unfolded clothes

UNFOLDED CLOTHES

CONTENTS

Acknowledgments

Chapter 1   UNFOLDED

Chapter 2   CLOTHES

UNFOLDED CLOTHES

ACKNOWLEDGMENTS

I like to say thank you to my mom Doris and my children Taijon, Diamond, Jyan and Seaven. To Bishop Tate thank you for laboring with me. To all my sisters thank you all for the encouragement, love, support, push and prayers.

Chapter 1

UNFOLDED

U.

***U**nderstanding the likes of a women neatly tucked away into smooth soft skin. Natural oils became perfumes of everyday talents; Her beauty realizes that her labor produces the sweetest fragrance.*

UNFOLDED CLOTHES

N.

_N_ever underestimate the co$t of her oil that is continually pouring out of her mind, unfolded to reveal a **light** that reflects the brightest wisdom taught by her Father.

UNFOLDED CLOTHES

F.

Future to a generation not yet *imagined*, tucked away is the plans locked in her thoughts, to birth a release that will take the breath of the taker.

O.

Opened ended instructions spoken in warrior's  dreams, beamed into the depths of her soul is a seed so small that it could be overtaken by emotions and drowned by broken tears

L.

*Leaving little space for unforgiveness, it shall **grow** to reach the highest point; to bring down **love** to a level of understanding that could be gripped by the weakest hand*

D.

Doubts murdered by the **sound** of growth, as she **stands** to reveal the height of **love** that **flows** from the top of her STANCE, that establish her position in the unproportioned land.

E.

***E**venly distributed throughout her being is the ability to handle what break's others so easily. Her back is strengthened by the hopes of a new tomorrow that circulates into today.*

D.

DRIfting words spoken from her Posture of humbleness brings her to a prominent place of the in between and the expansion of reality.

CHAPTER 2

CLOTHES...

UNFOLDED CLOTHES

C.

Cries of those **longing** for justice she holds in her hand and tosses them to catch **the** wind. Multiplying like **stars** is the spoken **letters** put together to become **prayers**.

UNFOLDED CLOTHES

L.

***L**ongevity is her preferred name as she lingers around to wipe away the residue of splattered tears.*

UNFOLDED CLOTHES

Often, she *is captivated, but not by the* **standards** *that so easily beset; But her captivity is by those who hold her freedom to unlock their chain of depravity.*

T.

*Though her pillow is that of a HIGHER place, her feet is hanging off the edge of the **earth**, she is well balanced in her life's affairs.*

H.

How is **she** so capable of *mastering* the **elements** that make up her existence? Balancing organized decks of **ideas** and *realism!*

UNFOLDED CLOTHES

E.

***E**laborate is the host of duties that pertains to* **femininity**, *the role that can be adjusted to fit ALL size situation.*

UNFOLDED CLOTHES

S.

Seemly super, o yes it seems as though SHE was **predestined** to BE a Phenomenal Superwoman, but to your surprise she leaves unfolded clothes to let you know that she is just only human

UNFOLDED CLOTHES

I Like to thank you for purchasing my book. I hope that it sparked your imagination and created a place for the Holy Spirit to minister to you. Please continue to the rest of the pages and let your creativity flow...enjoy.

UNFOLDED CLOTHES

This book in all its glory may not be duplicated for resell.

UNFOLDED CLOTHES

P.S....I am all about stretching a person to do to write ! Please use the remaining pages to write and draw your thoughts after reading this book.

HAVE FUN !

UNFOLDED CLOTHES

UNFOLDED CLOTHES

www.ingramcontent.com/pod-product-compliance
Lightning Source LLC
Chambersburg PA
CBHW060918050426
42453CB00010B/1799